THE BLITZ

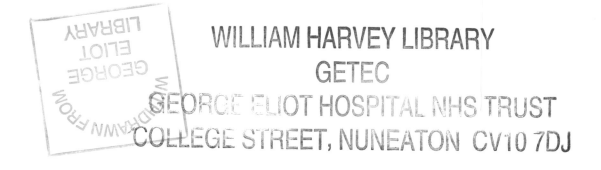

THE BLITZ

Maureen Hill

Photographs by the
Daily Mail

Bath · New York · Singapore · Hong Kong · Cologne · Delhi · Melbourne

This edition published by Parragon in 2010

Parragon
Queen Street House
4 Queen Street
Bath BA1 1HE, UK

All photographs © Associated Newspapers Ltd
Text © Parragon Books Ltd 2002
Produced by Atlantic Publishing

A catalogue record for this book is available
from the British Library.

ISBN: 978-1-4454-0847-7
Printed in China

*A small number of images within this book feature
graphic examples of the destruction caused by war.
Some people may find these disturbing.*

Introduction

War on the Home Front

On the third of September 1939 people all over Britain tuned in to their radios to hear Prime Minister Neville Chamberlain broadcast the fateful words 'as from eleven o'clock this morning Britain is at war with Germany'. It was not unexpected. For months Germany had been threatening the peace in Europe by its aggressive postures towards other sovereign nations. With the invasion of Poland, which Britain had agreed to protect, war was inevitable. It was a war which from the start drew in much of Europe and which was, over the next six years, to become a conflict of global proportions.

For the citizens of Britain on that morning in September there was only a dim understanding of how the war would affect their daily lives. There had been preparations for war from early in 1939. In March a Conscription Bill allowed for the registration of young men, ready for call-up if war was declared. Plans for coastal defences and the possibility of invasion were drawn up. Twelve regional Civil Defence commissioners were also appointed with special powers to govern their areas if they should become cut off from central government.

Many of the early Civil Defence measures were related to the threat of aerial bombardment. Air raid shelters were delivered to thousands of homes and plans were made to evacuate children and some women from areas thought to be at risk of bombing. There was a real fear that Luftwaffe planes would drop explosive, incendiary and poison gas bombs. In the months preceding the outbreak of war 38 million gas masks were distributed; there were Mickey Mouse-faced ones for young children and complete respirator suits for babies.

The Second World War would touch the lives of every one of the people listening to Chamberlain's broadcast in a way that was unprecedented in Britain. As in many previous wars those at home would have the anxieties and griefs over the fate of their loved ones at the front, but this time they would also be more directly and physically involved themselves. The nation's island geography helped protect it from invasion but also made it difficult to import the supplies on which a sophisticated economy like Britain's depended. Those on the 'home front' would have to fight a battle with shortages, using creativity and ingenuity to 'make do and mend'. But the greatest challenge to the home front was to be coping with the devastation, destruction and fear caused by the terrifying new tactic of war – aerial bombardment.

Blitz on Britain

The Blitz is the name given to a nine-month period of sustained aerial bombardment on British towns and cities during World War Two. However, there were air raids throughout the war; even when the Germans were on the run their High Command was able to attack the British Isles, late on in the war, using pilotless rocket bombs.

For the people of Britain who had listened anxiously to the announcement of war, there was to be a period of relative calm before the storm. It had been expected that within a short time of the declaration of war, German bombers would cloud the skies above the major cities raining bombs on the population below. With this in mind a mass evacuation of children, mothers of young babies, the sick and the infirm, took place in the first few weeks of the war. However, no raids came and many evacuees had drifted home by Christmas 1939.

The war was being fought by soldiers in Europe, although for much of the time there was an impasse, the 'phoney war'. When the German army made a lightning attack in April 1940 the British Expeditionary Force and Britain's allies were caught unprepared in the face of a force that Germany had been training and readying for five years. The blitzkrieg on Norway, Denmark, the Low Countries and France pushed back the BEF to the beaches of Dunkirk by late May 1940. The dramatic rescue of the majority of the men enabled the newly installed Prime Minister, Winston Churchill, to turn what could have been an ignominious defeat into a triumph of the British Spirit.

After Dunkirk, Germany prepared a plan, codenamed Operation Sea Lion, for the invasion of Britain. In order for the plan to succeed the Luftwaffe would have to destroy the RAF's capacity to mount a defence against troops invading from the sea. So began the Battle of Britain, fought in the hot summer of 1940 in the skies of Europe. The date set for the invasion was 15th September but by that time the RAF had defeated the Luftwaffe, downing so many of its planes that there would have been insufficient cover for the troopships of an invading army.

Calling off the invasion made the German High Command seek an alternative strategy to defeat Britain. The solution was aerial bombing which was intended to destroy the means of production of the weapons of war, while also causing such death and destruction that the British people would urge the government to sue for peace with Germany. It was a strategy the Allies would also adopt, leading to one of the most devastating bombing raids of the war when in February 1945 the German city of Dresden was virtually destroyed.

On 7th September 1940, the Blitz began in earnest. Throughout the Battle of Britain many south-east towns, including the capital itself, had suffered bombing from German aircraft as the Luftwaffe attempted to destroy ground air defences as well as the RAF. During this period there were also glimpses of the use of aerial terror tactics on the civilian population as bombs were dropped on non-military targets or machine gunners strafed public areas. In September, with the failure of Operation Sea Lion, these tactics became German policy.

The first raid hit London during the daylight hours of a beautiful, sunny September day. Hundreds of incendiary bombs were dropped on the dock area and the fires they started provided a guide and target for the night-time raiders. All night the Luftwaffe bombed the East End and by morning there were 430 civilians dead, 1600 injured and thousands made homeless. The raids on London continued every night for the next 55 days, although after the first week most raids took place under cover of darkness as the Germans found their losses too great with daylight raids.

Casualties in London for September and October were high – 13,000 killed and 20,000 injured. However, the availability of deep shelters in the Underground system helped reduce the numbers. Tube stations became the preferred shelters for Londoners, although initially the authorities were averse to the system being used for this purpose, believing it would seriously compromise the Underground's ability to function. There were also fears that the population would develop a 'deep shelter mentality', making it difficult to carry on as normally as possible. Public demand, and the clear evidence that the city and its people could still function, changed the government's mind.

During the closing months of 1940 life for most Londoners became a relentless routine of going into shelters as dusk fell, sleeping or dozing through the night, listening to the raids outside and emerging in the morning to see the extent of the damage. Days were spent at work, or clearing up the remains of bombed homes and workplaces, or trying to look after a family at home. Those made homeless tried to carry on their lives in temporary accommodation in public buildings such as church halls and schools.

At the very end of the year, London was hit by one of the most devastating raids of the war. It was Sunday night, 29th December, and the Thames was at its lowest ebb. High explosive parachute mines severed the water mains at the beginning of the raid, during which more than 10,000 incendiary bombs were dropped on the City of London. The result was the second Fire of London. Twenty thousand firefighters, assisted by countless soldiers, using 2,300 pumps to take water directly from the river, fought to control the blaze which threatened to turn the City into one huge conflagration.

May 11th 1941 marked the end of the sustained aerial assault on London until the terror raids of the V1 and V2 pilotless rocket bombs in 1944. On that Spring night over 500 Luftwaffe aircraft dropped hundreds of high explosive bombs and tens of thousands of incendiary devices. Many London landmarks were hit, including the chamber of the House of Commons, Big Ben, Westminster Abbey, the Guildhall and the British Museum, where a quarter of a million books were destroyed.

London, as the symbolic as well as administrative and economic heart of the nation, was clearly a target but from the first weeks of the Blitz other towns and cities across Britain were also under attack. Some, like the ancient cathedral city of Coventry, suffered nights of bombing just as intense as those on the capital. After a raid on 14th November 1940 Coventry's cathedral was reduced almost entirely to rubble, along with many other buildings in the city centre. A squad of 400 Luftwaffe bombers had dropped 600 tons of high explosives and thousands of incendiaries.

Many cities and towns throughout Britain were targeted as important industrial centres where the weapons of war were produced, from small ordnance to tanks and anti-aircraft guns. Other coastal areas were major naval ports, building both war and merchant ships at one point of the war at the rate of one per week. Hardly a town of any size escaped aerial assault throughout the war. Many, like Liverpool, Manchester, Bristol, Birmingham and Southampton suffered nights of severe bombing. During November and December 1940 each of these cities was prey to a favoured German tactic of a heavy raid one night followed by a further heavy raid either the following night or very soon after.

At the end of June 1941, Hitler broke a non-aggression pact he had signed before the war with the Soviet Union and invaded Russia. Bombing in Britain had petered out in May as the Germans prepared for the attack on Russia and the demands of fighting the war on a new front kept the Luftwaffe from being able to mount the level of bombing it had done for that frightening period from September 1940 to May 1941. Air raids continued but infrequently, often as reprisals for the RAF bombing of German targets.

Later on, in 1942, a new tactic emerged in the bombing pattern as a response to the effects of devastating bombing of Germany by the RAF. This time, instead of targeting major industrial centres, less heavily protected towns and cities were chosen in an attempt to cause most public distress. These towns appear to have been selected from their entries in Baedeker's travel guide to Britain and the subsequent raids became known as the 'Baedeker raids'. Consequently the targets included some of the most beautiful and historic towns in Britain – Exeter, Bath, Norwich and York.

Even the destruction of these ancient towns did not demoralise the British public; indeed it had almost the reverse effect, helping to contribute to a sense of a nation pulling together. The bombing affected everyone's life, ranging from the simple inconveniences of the Blackout and other air raid precautions, to the loss of homes, landmarks and lives, to the constant fear of attack which was a reality for young and old, rich and poor, town or country dweller.

Many of the most memorable images of the war come from the assault on Britain by Luftwaffe bombers. This book selects some of those images from the *Daily Mail* archive, photographs taken at the time, now renovated to original quality. Together they provide an impressionistic collage of life at that time, showing the devastation and destruction wreaked by aerial bombardment but also celebrating the ability of the human spirit to cope and survive in times of extreme stress.

Before the Blitz

Opposite: The Queen visits the wounded and widows from the Battle of the River Plate. In December 1939 three British cruisers - Ajax, Achilles and Exeter - battled with the Graf Spee which had been harassing merchant shipping, forcing the German pocket battleship into Montevideo harbour where she was scuttled by her crew.

Top right: An RAF man examines the wreckage of one of the engines from a German mine-laying plane which crashed in Clacton with a full load of mines destined for the North Sea shipping lanes in May 1940.

Bottom right: Shops in Surrey wrecked by bombs dropped in a raid during the Battle of Britain.

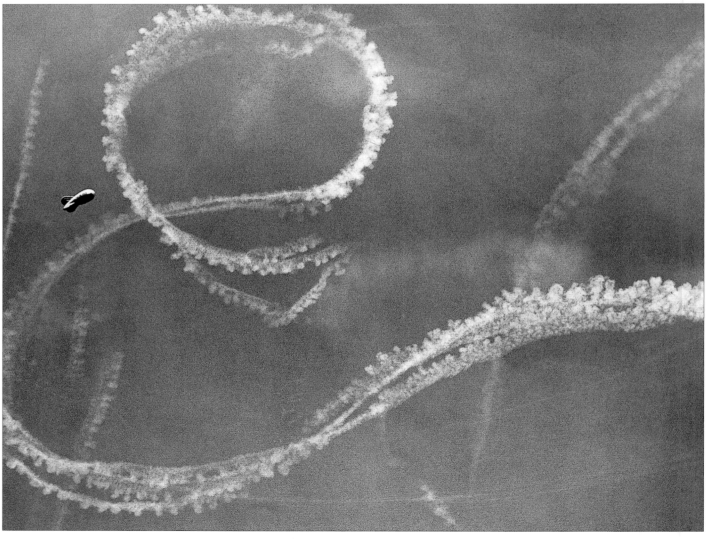

Battle of Britain

Opposite top: A German raider dodges a barrage balloon while being chased by a British fighter which brought the bomber down shortly after this picture was taken. The raider had just dropped his bombs over the south-east coast. South-coast areas suffered the worst bombing prior to the Blitz, as the Germans tried to destroy ground air defences during the Battle of Britain.

Opposite below: Over the Dover coast, British fighter planes leave twisting vapour trails as they engage enemy aircraft in dog-fights.

Right: Bombs exploding on Folkestone.

Below: The result of a fierce attack on Ramsgate at the end of August, as Germany tried desperately to gain air supremacy.

Anderson Shelters offer protection

Opposite top: Mrs E Cullen was protected by her Anderson Shelter when a bomb fell nearby during a German raid that reached the south-west suburbs of London.

Opposite below: This Anderson Shelter was riddled with machine gun fire from a low-flying German plane during the same raid.

Right: These men were not put off their pints when the blast from a bomb knocked out the pub window.

Below: Some of the Battle of Britain raids reached as far as the heart of London. Here the statue of the poet John Milton was knocked off its pedestal in St Giles Church, Cripplegate.

Suburbs clear up

Above: A Sunday morning in August 1940 and the clear-up begins after the previous night's raid on this London suburb.

Right: Workers queue to have their identity cards inspected by Police following a raid on the City. One of the early effects of the war was a restriction on some of the freedoms enjoyed by the British people. Identity cards were issued and certain areas became restricted for access. For example, in the weeks before the D Day landings visitors were banned from going within 10 miles of the coast from The Wash to Land's End.

Opposite: Burlington Arcade was damaged in one of the first bombing raids of the Blitz.

Oxford Street hit

Above: John Lewis's department store was hit during one of the early raids in the Blitz in September 1940. By this time shops were having a difficult time keeping their shelves stocked. Food rationing had begun in January but clothing was not rationed until June 1941.

Right: Firefighters play their hoses on the National Bank, just along the road from John Lewis's.

Opposite: At Oxford Circus, Peter Robinson's department store was hit during the same raid. That night, 18th September, saw damage to the Inner Temple library and County Hall, as well as several major shops.

Time bomb damages Buckingham Palace

Right and below: The King and Queen inspect the damage done to Buckingham Palace when a time bomb, dropped by a German raider, went off inside the grounds in September 1940. The damaged building had been specially converted to house a swimming pool for Princess Elizabeth and Princess Margaret.

The Royal Family remained in residence throughout the war, suffering the privations of the Blackout and the dangers associated with the bombing. Buckingham Palace was hit several times.

Opposite: Prime Minister Winston Churchill joins the King and Queen as they tour the wreckage at the Palace. Photographs like this one helped boost public morale as people felt that those in authority shared their fears and problems - it prompted reports such as 'The Royal Family are one with their subjects in London's time of trial.'

Bond Street bombed

Right: The scene in Bond Street the morning after a raid in September 1940.

Above: Workmen repair damage to the roadway outside Buckingham Palace, the result of a bomb which fell just outside the Palace gates. There was a popular belief that the Luftwaffe were deliberately targeting the residence of the monarch.

Opposite top: A line of wrecked taxi cabs, parked ironically outside the Automobile Association's offices in Leicester Square. Note the repair lorry from the 'Gas light and Coke Company' attending the scene to prevent further damage from gas explosions.

Opposite below: Ruined buildings in Leicester Square, damaged when a bomb dropped directly into the square.

Sniffing out danger!

A policeman checks for gas leaking from this street lamp following a daylight raid in October 1940. Gas explosions and fires following a bombing raid were a constant hazard and required vigilance on the part of the public and Civil Defence personnel.

Opposite top: Damaged trams in a London street following a raid. The capital lost so many buses and trams in the Blitz that buses were drafted in from the provinces. The familiar red buses were supplemented by several other hues.

Opposite below: As was often the case, the Police were first on the scene after the raid, taking charge, directing people away from danger and calling up rescue services.

She saved the X-ray equipment

Right: This doctor's assistant managed to salvage the X-ray equipment when the clinic in Harley Street was bombed.

Below: Vapour trails from a dog-fight early in the Blitz. The majority of the early raids took place by day, but German losses were large and soon the Luftwaffe changed tactics to night-time bombing.

Opposite top left: The scene after a night raid - the force of one explosion hurled this bus, upended, against a wall.

Opposite top right: Bombed-out Londoners sleep in a shelter where they are accommodated until new homes can be found for them.

Opposite below: The wreckage of a seamen's home and a hotel in Dover caused by a combined attack from long-range guns fired from the French coast and German bomber aircraft. Two American reporters were injured in the hotel.

Pegasus flies!

Right: As demolition workers pull down the tower of the Temple Library, made unsafe by bombing, the figure of Pegasus which topped the tower flies off.

Below: A family uses a handbarrow to remove the belongings they have managed to salvage from the wreckage of their bombed home.

Opposite top left: Workmen set about repairs to a bomb crater in the Strand, close to St Mary-le-Strand church.

Opposite top right: People in the street outside their ruined homes, collect together whatever belongings they can.

Opposite below: Women, made homeless in the raids, carry salvaged items, including milk and sugar, to a temporary shelter.

King and Queen tour East End

Amid the debris from a bombed London hospital the Queen paid tribute to the hospital workers, some of whom had been bombed out of their homes and yet continued to work long shifts on the wards.

Opposite: The Queen talks to East Enders after a night of severe bombing in which Buckingham Palace also suffered damage.

Victims

Right: Two Ambulance workers who have given immediate first aid to these women help them away from the scene.

Below: Physically unharmed but no less victims of the bombing, these people gather round their belongings.

Opposite top left: A City worker manages a smile after being rescued from a wrecked building.

Opposite top right: A woman sits on her doorstep with her young children and weeps after a night of heavy bombing on the East End.

Opposite below: Queuing for water from a standpipe after a raid. Raids usually knocked out essential services like water, electricity and gas, so people had to cope with temporary measures until repairs could be effected.

'Hitler's bombs can't beat us'

This greengrocery barrow carries on as usual amid the bombed ruins of a London street. The sign claims the oranges on sale have come through 'Musso's (Mussolini's) Lake', the Mediterranean Sea.

Opposite: Londoners try to get some sleep on the escalators of an Underground station. The noise of the raid may have been muffled but the wooden treads of the escalators would not have made for a very comfortable night's sleep.

Refugees

Right: A Warden helps these East End women and their belongings to safety after they were made homeless by the bombing.

Once homeless there was little choice of accommodation. Sometimes people could be put up by relatives or evacuated, and spare private rented property was used by councils to house a few of those who lost their homes. But most people spent at least some time temporarily housed in public buildings such as church halls and schools.

Below: Soldier volunteers from the Royal Army Pay Corps clear up in Harley Street. The Pioneer Corps, many of whom were recruited from the ranks of the unemployed at the beginning of the war, were charged with the task of salvage and clearing up, but it was such a huge job that many other civilian or military volunteers were required.

Opposite: A man makes his way to work down a blitzed Bruton Street.

Regent Street

Opposite top: A view down Regent Street towards Piccadilly Circus after a bombing raid. The crowd are held behind a cordon at the end of the road, safe from the dangers of falling masonry, gas explosions or unexploded bombs.

Opposite bottom: This tram in Blackfriars Road was damaged during a daylight raid.

Right: The Regent Palace hotel suffered in a raid in October 1940.

Below: Closer detail of the damage in the Regent Street area after a single night's bombing. Note the Air Raid Shelter signs on the building. All public buildings, including shops, had to provide a shelter or indicate where the nearest was located.

Birmingham bombed

Opposite right: Women, carrying their salvaged belongings, leave their bombed-out homes in this Birmingham street.

Opposite left: A nurse tends to her charges in what has become the dormitory of this ruined London orphanage.

Opposite below: Clear-up in Birmingham.

On 22nd November the city, targeted as an important industrial base, was hit by an 11-hour raid. Damage to the water systems created huge problems for firefighters trying to contain the fires. Water had to be pumped from the city's canals and in some cases fires had to be left to burn out.

Right: A District Line train still runs, despite the fact that the tunnel roof has collapsed.

Below: A ruined street in Stepney, East London.

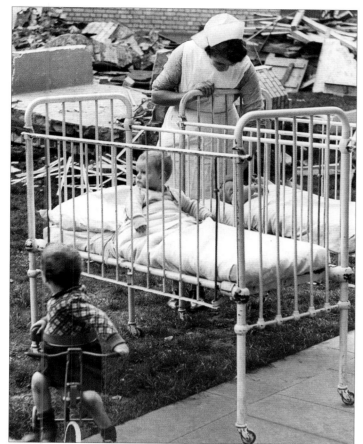

Coventry's Blitz

Opposite top: The spire of Coventry Cathedral rises above the ruined city centre. The body of the cathedral was destroyed, along with many other buildings during a devastating raid on 14th November 1940.

Opposite below: Pedestrians pick their way through the smouldering debris of Coventry city centre as they resume their daily lives.

Right: Midnight and firefighters tackle a blaze in Hatton Garden, Holborn.

Below: Smouldering ruins, including a burnt-out bus, in a Coventry street after the November raid. It is notable that most of the damage in the majority of air raids was caused, not by the impact of high explosive devices, but by the fires they started or incendiary bombs dropped with the specific objective of starting fires.

King visits Coventry

Above: King George visited the city of Coventry three days after the raid to see for himself the damage caused. He was accompanied by Herbert Morrison (behind, in glasses) who was Minister for Home Security at the time.

Right: Rescue workers bring out a Mr Newman from a bombed building after he was buried under debris for 14 hours. Apart from suffering from shock, he was unharmed.

Opposite top: Only the chimney stacks are left standing in what was once a busy shopping street in the centre of Coventry.

Opposite below: A picture taken on the morning after the Coventry raid shows debris in the foreground while firefighters struggle to control the flames in a still-burning building.

Restoring communications in Southampton

Opposite top left: A soldier assists a civilian worker to restore communications in Southampton which had been severed during an attack. As a major naval base, Southampton was always a target, but at the end of November and the beginning of December, it was hit by a series of severe raids.

Opposite top right: This rather unusual photograph was taken in the debris of the dining hall of the Inner Temple, London, where the figures of Crusaders and Knights Templar originally provided the decoration.

Opposite below: Members of the Pioneer Corps help Londoners salvage their belongings.

Above: Coventry city centre after the bombing.

Left: King George inspects the devastation in Coventry Cathedral.

Bristol bombed

Right: The King inspects bomb damage in Bristol on a visit in mid-December 1940. Earlier in the month the city had been hit by two major attacks.

Below: Nurses meet the King on his tour of the city. The Bristol Children's Hospital was hit during one of the raids, but with few casualties.

Opposite top: Citizens of Bristol welcome the King.

Opposite below left: Mrs Beatrice Herbert meets the King standing on the wreckage of the home from which she escaped.

Opposite below right: The Dutch House, a centuries-old landmark in Bristol, after the raids.

'Tea-total warfare'

Below: Shelterers in the Tube at Holland Park are served tea or coffee as a night-cap before they settle down in the station for the night. This was a new service inaugurated by the government and the London Transport Board.

Right: A London building ablaze as firefighters struggle to bring the flames under control.

Opposite top: Princess Galitzine of the exiled Russian Royal Family was killed when this bus was hit during an air raid.

Opposite below: Damage to The Oval, Surrey County Cricket Club's ground, after an enemy bomb dropped nearby.

Largest bomb crater in London

Opposite: The largest bomb crater in London, created when a bomb made a direct hit on the ticket hall of Bank Tube Station. At least fifty people were killed among the travelling public and those entering the station for the night's shelter.

Right: The Union Jack still flies across the entrance to the Langham Hotel, just a short distance from Broadcasting House, HQ of the BBC.

Below: During an operation to clear the furniture from this bombed house the photographer captured the reactions when another enemy plane flew overhead. The neighbours and home owners looked up warily; the Civil Defence workers carried on as usual - they were accustomed to working under such conditions.

Manchester Cathedral damaged

Below: Damage caused to Manchester Cathedral during heavy raids on the city on 23rd and 24th December 1940.

Right: Children's toys are among the items being salvaged from this North London suburban home.

Opposite: A bomb crater inside St Paul's Cathedral. The high explosive device fell through the roof before crashing into the crypt where it detonated.

One of the most enduring images of the war is of St Paul's Cathedral rising intact above the burning City, as if in affirmation of the spirit to survive. However, it did suffer damage on more than one occasion during the war. In October 1940, a bomb destroyed the High Altar but did no damage to any other part of the building.

Spirit of Plymouth

Below: After a third successive night of bombing a group of Plymouth's citizens gather around a salvaged piano for a song.

Right: Not all creatures rescued from the bomb ruins were human. Here the special squad run by ARP, together with members of the People's Dispensary for Sick Animals (PDSA), save a dog that had been buried for four days.

Opposite top left: A bomb crater just inside the railings of Buckingham Palace.

Opposite top right: In the same raid a corner of the Palace was damaged, destroying this bedroom.

Opposite below: When a bomb blew a hole in the road outside Blackfriars Station trains continued to run while the repairs were carried out overhead.

Liverpool's Christmas Blitz

Above and opposite: The debris in Liverpool after the demolition squad had made the area safe after raids. Liverpool and the Birkenhead area suffered two nights of heavy attack on 20th and 21st December 1940. Over two hundred people lost their lives.

Right: Mrs Wingrave from London retrieves a picture from her bombed-out home. She and her family escaped injury when the bomb dropped as they were in their air raid shelter.

Sheffield's trams destroyed

Opposite below: Wrecked tramcars in a Sheffield street after a severe attack on the city on 12th December 1940 in which virtually every tram sustained damage and 31 were totally destroyed.

Opposite top: Soldiers clear up damage to Northcliffe House, the *Daily Mail* building, in Manchester.

Right: Salvaging from a shop in the centre of Birmingham's shopping district.

Below: This car was unable to stop and fell into a bomb crater. Driving in the Blackout was fraught with dangers. Car headlights were dim and had to illuminate only a short distance in front. Added to that was the fact that no light could escape from buildings and that street lamps were either not in use or only very dimly lit.

In the first few weeks of the Blackout there was a huge increase in deaths and injuries on the road.

Spiritual help among the ruins

Right: A nun, a parishioner and child kneel in prayer among the ruins of a bombed London church.

Below: St George's Roman Catholic Cathedral, Southwark carries on the work of the Church despite the fact that the roof and all the internal fittings have been destroyed by incendiary bombs.

Opposite top: A street in central Plymouth after a raid. Like Southampton, Plymouth was targeted as an important naval base. The city, despite being extensively damaged, managed to keep running as normally as possible.

Opposite below: The city centre of Manchester which suffered severe raids in the run-up to Christmas 1940.

City devastated by second great fire

Above: On New Year's Day 1941, the Lord Mayor of London inspects the damage in Aldermanbury, following on from the most devastating raid of the war to date. On 29th December, when the Thames was at its lowest ebb, Luftwaffe bombers had hit the water mains before dropping more than 10,000 incendiaries. More than 20,000 fire fighters were reinforced by soldiers and civilians in an attempt to prevent the City being turned into an inferno.

Right: St Anne's Parochial School, Hatton Garden, ablaze as fire fighters struggle to bring the flames under control.

Opposite: The Pioneer Corps clear up in the area around the Tower following on from the raid.

London carries on

Opposite top right: The Guildhall in use after fire destroyed its roof and damaged much of the stained glass. The election of Sheriff takes place under a temporary roof.

Opposite top left: A building collapses after being dynamited in an attempt to make it safe. Demolition squads were often aided by Royal Engineers who helped lay the charges.

Opposite below left: A cheeky verse in defiance of the bombers.

Opposite below right: Big Ben's scarred face still tells the time under gashed and splintered masonry.

Right: The roof of a tramcar lies in the road of this Liverpool street - just another obstacle for the pedestrians to negotiate their way around.

Below: Damage to one of the rooms housing skulls and skeletons at the Royal College of Surgeons in London.

West End wrecked

Wreckage strews the roadway in the famous London thoroughfare of Jermyn Street.

Opposite top: London's Queen Victoria Street, with the ruined church of St Nicholas Cole Abbey in the centre, carries on as usual, despite the war damage.

Opposite below: Rows of blackened skulls and skeletons form a strange image in a gallery damaged by fire at the Royal College of Surgeons.

Sleeping in the Underground

Above: Passengers on the platform wait for the last train while others settle down to sleep in their bunks. After initial reticence on the part of the authorities Underground stations became favoured shelters for blitzed Londoners and eventually bunks were installed on platforms.

Right: These children settle down in hammocks slung between the rails at Aldwych station.

Opposite: The largest bomb crater in London was spanned by a temporary road bridge and the troops who had constructed it were permitted to take the first ride across it. The censor only allowed this picture to be published on condition that the crater was blacked out.

Middlesbrough Station hit hard

Right and opposite top left: The wreckage inside and outside Middlesbrough Railway Station after a raid.

Above: Plymouth, viewed from the top of the ruined Guildhall tower, shows its scars after the clear-up operation begins.

Opposite below left: Salvaging household goods after a raid on Exeter.

Opposite right: Demolition work required skill and a great deal of nerve! This man balances precariously atop a ruined chimney stack to make it safe for others. The bricks would be reclaimed and reused to repair other damaged buildings.

Deep tunnel shelters

Right: German bombing became a much less frequent occurrence after May 1941 when Hitler turned his attention to the Eastern Front and the attack on the Soviet Union. Nevertheless, it was still necessary to prepare for air raids. In 1942 several deep shelters were built below London Tube Stations.

Below: Two women pick their way through the debris of an Exeter street after a so-called 'Baedeker raid' - a series of raids in 1942 which targeted historic cities like York, Bath and Norwich selected from the Baedeker Guide book.

Opposite: St Paul's intact amid the devastation of the surrounding streets.

Baedeker raids

Right: The gutted interior of a church in the city of Bath, hit during a series of raids on historic British towns selected from their entries in the Baedeker travel guide book.

Below: These people were made homeless in a raid on Canterbury in June 1942 - another city targeted in the 'Baedeker raids'.

Opposite top: Troops and civilian workers clear up debris in a Canterbury street.

Opposite below: Firefighters at work in Holborn during the last major raid on London in May 1941 in the main period of the Blitz.

The censor did not release this picture for publication until February 1942.

Images were kept from publication for a variety of reasons but the two principal ones were, firstly, to ensure that the enemy did not gain details of the areas hit and so allow assessment of the accuracy of their bombing and, secondly, to avoid damaging public morale with scenes too devastating or distressing.

Mystery explosion at Elephant and Castle

Right: An unexplained explosion at this house causes concern among the residents.

Even after bombing raids there was always a fear of explosion. Sometimes German planes dropped time bombs which would detonate hours or days after a raid, sometimes a bomb would bury itself in the ground and remain unexploded for months before something set it off unexpectedly.

Below: Wreckage in the streets of Southampton. The fire hoses are still out and the ruins smoulder on the morning after the raid.

Opposite: London's St Bride Street on the morning after a raid. Most of the people on the street are on their way to work. Many would find their work place destroyed and would have to set about the task of salvaging what they could and moving to alternative accommodation before beginning the task of reconstructing the business. It became a matter of national pride to be able to proclaim 'Business as usual'.

A home in the street

Right: Rubble and salvaged household items from someone's home lie in this Canterbury street after a lightning raid by German aircraft in November 1942.

Below: Despite the damage to the fabric of the church the work of the clergy goes on. The congregation stand in the aisles below a makeshift altar.

Opposite: St Paul's Cathedral seen from a new vista. After the relentless raids of the Blitz, particularly the major raid of December 1940 which caused devastating fires in the surrounding area, St Paul's was revealed. Many of the ancient and narrow streets which crowded around it were so damaged that they had to be demolished for safety's sake.

Manchester's Victoria dome bombed-out

Right: The damaged dome of the Victoria Building in Manchester's city centre rises above the ruins created by the bombing.

Below: Londoners all smiles despite being bombed-out of their home after a raid which came in July 1941 after a lull in the bombing campaign. Note the 'V' for victory sign chalked on the wall, adopted from Prime Minister Winston Churchill's famous two-fingered salute.

Opposite: Dressed smartly and smiling, women make their way to work over the bomb rubble from the previous night's raid.

Homeless on Clydebank

Right: A family made homeless by air raids targeting the shipbuilding industry on the Clyde leave their shattered street.

Below: Damaged buses in the bus station at Dover caused by an air raid, but the town was also prey to attack from German long-range guns stationed on the French coast.

Opposite top: PC Robert Cross, with his eye bandaged, removes furniture from his bombed-out home after a raid in late 1943.

Opposite below left and right: Salvaging from homes in the London area.

Time for tea

Opposite: Four boys take tea in the garden of their damaged home after a daylight raid in March 1943.

Right: These children were made homeless during a 'Baedeker raid' on the city of Norwich. They are being cared for at a rest centre established by the London County Council. Many local authorities would send aid to other areas when they were hit particularly hard by bombing and the home area services were overwhelmed.

Below: The Salvation Army administer tea and sympathy to Mrs F Bush who had been rescued after being buried under the debris of her home.

Coastal raid

Right: Damage to a bus during a daylight raid on a south-coast town in June 1943.

Below: Richard the Lionheart escaped with only a bent sword when a bomb dropped on the Houses of Parliament.

Opposite top: Another daylight raid on a south-east town in the summer of 1943. By this time the war was going badly for the Germans. They had lost ground in North Africa, the Ruhr dams had been breached by British bombers, German U-boats in the Atlantic were losing supremacy, German tank divisions had been smashed at Kursk and the Allies were on their way to victory in Italy.

Opposite below: Manchester United's stadium after a bomb had dropped through the roof of the main stand.

Business as usual

Right: A messenger tries to puzzle out the new addresses of firms that have lost their premises due to the bombing.

Below: The St George's area of Canterbury after the clean-up operation. People go about their daily lives on foot, by bicycle, bus, even in horse-drawn carts as the city gets back to 'business as usual'.

Opposite: Queen Victoria Street with a new view of St Paul's after the demolition and clear-up have removed unsafe bombed buildings.

The spirit of the Blitz

In many ways this picture captures the essence of Britain during the Blitz - the bomb damage, the shelter signs, the poster urging donations to the Spitfire Fund, the community spirit of the residents chatting on a street corner, and the spirit of defiance, the urge to 'Keep - Smiling'.

A symbol of survival

St Paul's Cathedral rises above the smoke and flames of one of the worst nights of bombing experienced in Britain. On 29th December 1940 when the Thames was at low water mark and after the early bombing run had severed the water mains, the Luftwaffe's aircraft dropped more than 10,000 incendiary bombs on the City. By some miracle the landmark church and its dome remained untouched as thousands of firefighters and troops fought to prevent the ancient heart of London being destroyed by an inferno.

Opposite: Getting back to normal, as the crater outside Bank is mended, the temporary structure removed so that traffic can begin to flow more freely.

ACKNOWLEDGEMENTS

The photographs in this book are from the archives of the *Daily Mail*.
Particular thanks to Steve Torrington, Dave Sheppard, Brian Jackson,
Alan Pinnock, Paul Rossiter, Richard Jones and all the staff.

Thanks also to Cliff Salter, Richard Betts, Liz Balmer,
Peter Wright, Trevor Bunting and Simon Taylor.
Design by John Dunne.